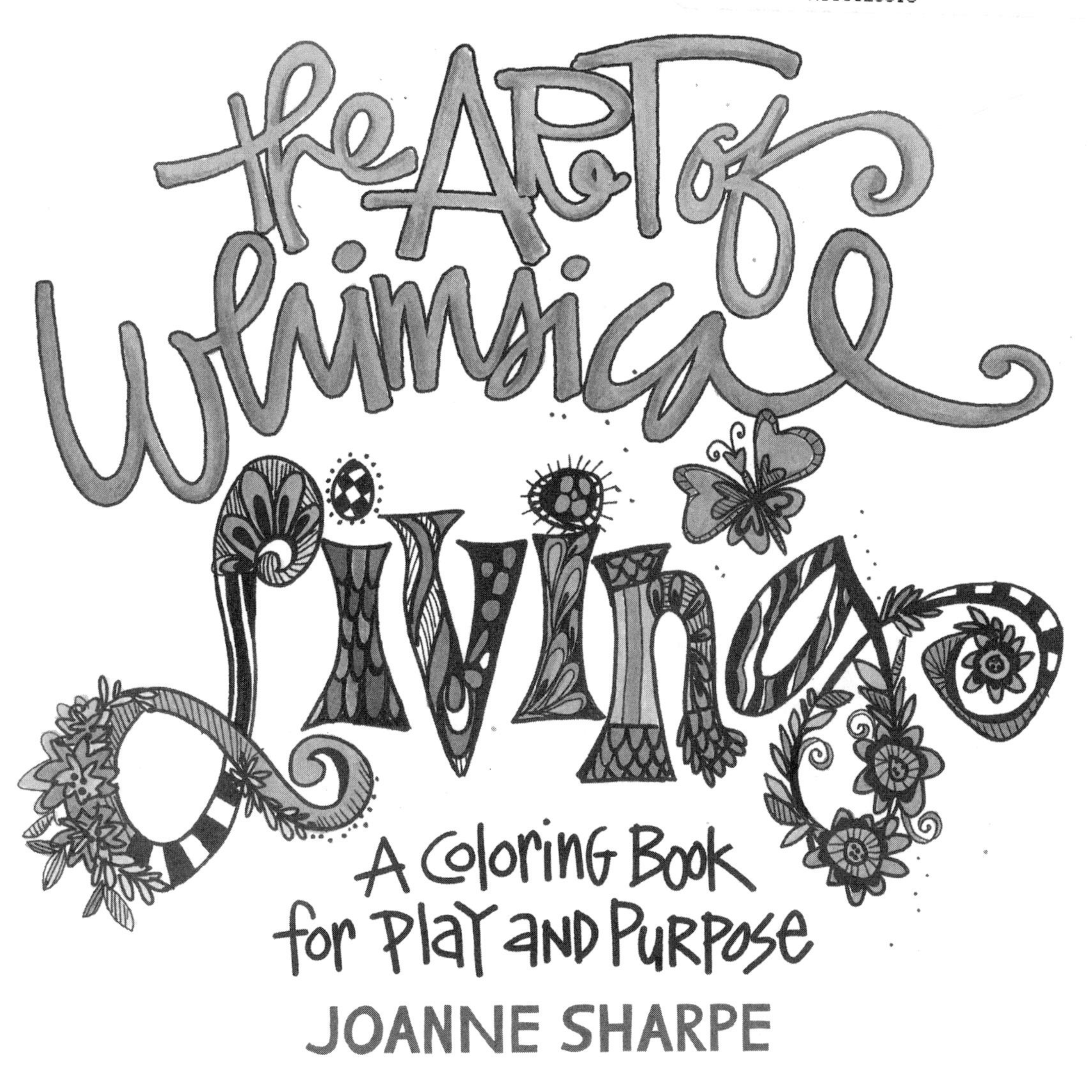

JOANNE SHARPE

NORTH LIGHT BOOKS
CINCINNATI, OHIO
clothpaperscissors.com

Contents

Live each day with Passion and Purpose

the COLOR-LOVING LIFE

There is no shortage of coloring book choices on the market today. Who doesn't love to color? For my entire life, coloring has been a favorite pastime as well as a constant element in much of my artwork. Whether I am using marker, paintbrush or colored pencil, coloring gives life to my drawings and design. In this, my debut coloring book, I offer a collection of art that provides you the opportunity for coloring with purpose—an interactive collection of art to be personalized, customized and shared.

Here you will find energetic, whimsical art to color to make every day a colorful masterpiece. Make all the details of your every day a bit more colorful using the imagery on these pages to illustrate each task or message. Make your own gifts, organize your thoughts and activities, document your days or plan your tasks on these pages using your own personal color stories.

Each page is perforated so you can tear out the original and use the art for multiple purposes, saving it to be used over and over again. Use your home printer or a retail copy shop to reproduce the art pages to suit all your creative coloring ideas.

follow
your
Bliss

MANTRAS

A mantra is defined as a repeated expression or idea, most commonly used in meditation. To me, it's usually a simple phrase that nurtures a desired mindset, response or feeling. Make your mantras while coloring art.

- Use the mantra pages to make a collection of colorful life reminders or to share with others.
- Change the size of the original page art and print out assorted sizes, large and small, and color with different color stories, such as cool blues, warm reds, oranges, yellows or hot colors like pink, lime-green and turquoise. Different color schemes can evoke specific feelings and emotional responses.

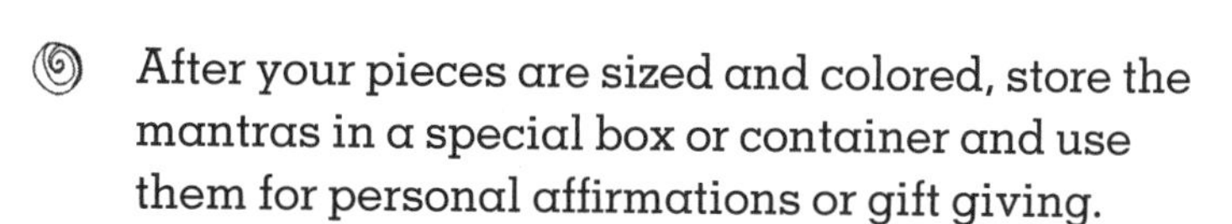

- After your pieces are sized and colored, store the mantras in a special box or container and use them for personal affirmations or gift giving.
- Display a favorite mantra taped to a mirror or your car dashboard.
- Color and frame a specific mantra as a personal visual inspiration or give one as a gift.

It's
All

All is Well

Be a
Joy
Maker.

Count your blessings

Your Heart Knows

You are loved

imagine
the
possibilities

Let it Go

TODAYS
THE
DAY

follow
Your
BLiSS

Every
Moment
Matters

Keep the Faith

HAPPY
BIRTHDAY

NOTES and MESSAGE CARDS

In this technical, electronic culture we live in, there is something very special about a handmade, heartfelt card or gift. Put your coloring to practical use by creating your own line of colorful greeting cards. Be creative with your techniques, using the art in different sizes and boldly coloring with assorted art supplies like ink pens, watercolor paints and sparkly, glittering gel pens.

- Scan the art from the book page and print onto cardstock before coloring (and sharing!).

- Enlarge or reduce the page art and print onto watercolor paper. Trim the art to create a one-sided panel card and color with water-soluble colored pencils or watercolor paints. Paste the art onto decorative cardstock to create an original masterpiece for gifting.

- Make assorted sizes of the message cards to color and cut. Fussy-cut around the outline edges to make an interesting dimensional shape.

- Keep a stack of these cards ready to personalize and distribute to your family and friends. Tuck them in a lunchbox, mailbox or tote bag as a surprise for your family and special friends. These are great to give to kids and students. Print the message cards on paper and color with your favorite tools.

- Share the love, inspire and touch the world! Print in small sizes, cut and color and leave the happy message cards in public places as surprises to be found by unknowing strangers.

You are so Loved

Be Epic

thinking
of You
today

You
GOT
this

You're
PRETTY
AWESOME!

You're
MY
Superstar

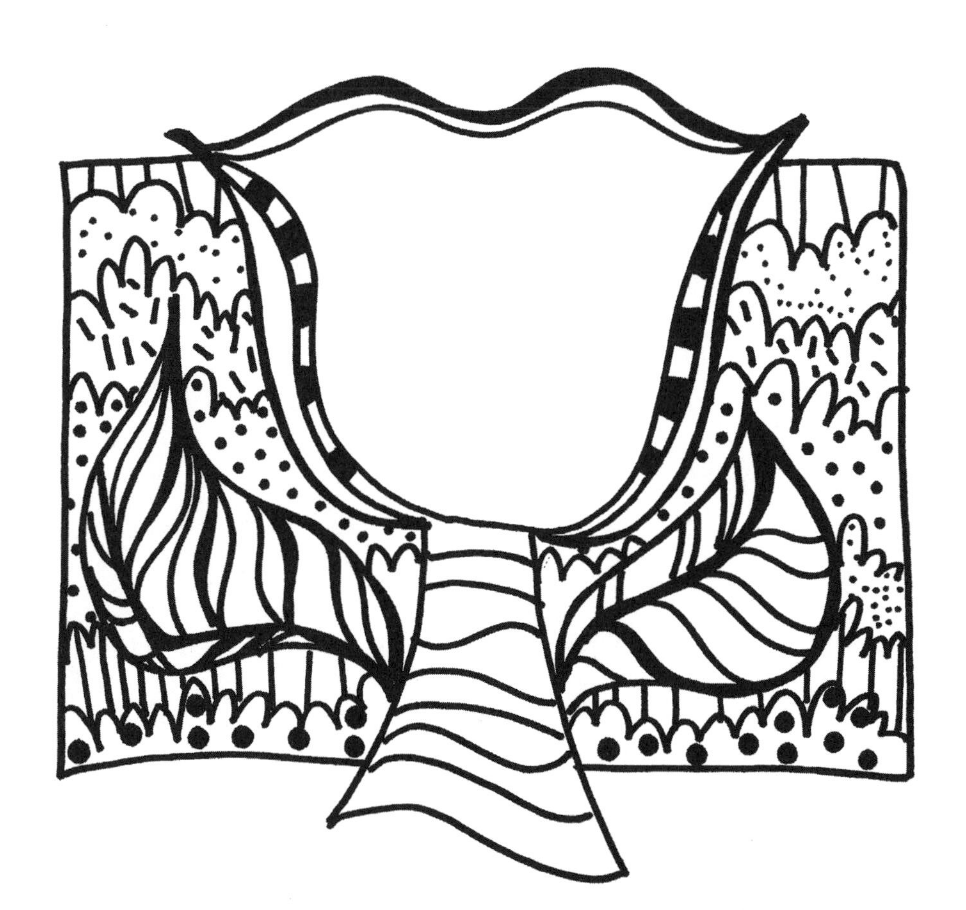

Happy
Birthday

HAPPY
HAPPY
BIRTH
DAY

Congrats to you!

happy birthday to you

thinking
of you

thank
you

hello

thanks so much

get well soon

FEEL BETTER

NOVEMBER
SUNDAY
MONDAY
TUESDAY
WEDNESDAY
THURSDAY
FRIDAY
SATURDAY

CALENDARS

Do you have a favorite calendar you use every year?
Put your coloring skills in motion to create
your own in your favorite custom colors.

- Take advantage of these monthly pages at full size. Color with your favorite markers and use seasonal colors for each month. At home, this is perfect fridge art, displayed prominently with magnets for easy access and everyday view.

- Copy, bind and gift large or small versions of the calendar for a specific audience like grandparents, college kids, teachers, etc.

- Make your personal or family calendar mini and portable. Take the master sheets to a copy shop, reduce the page size and have them printed on cardstock . Have the sheets assembled with a coil or plastic binding to flip the pages. These are perfect for carrying in a purse or tote bag so you can color on the go.

- Customize and create a "Birthday Calendar" for family and friends. Copy and print one master copy of all twelve months. On the master, hand-letter the birthday dates of every family member in each month. Make enough copies, spiral-bound and uncolored, to distribute to each family member. Everyone will enjoy coloring his or her own calendar to remember special dates.

JANUARY
SUNDAY
MONDAY
TUESDAY
WEDNESDAY
THURSDAY
FRIDAY
SATURDAY

February
SUNDAY
MONDAY
TUESDAY
WEDNESDAY
THURSDAY
FRIDAY
SATURDAY

MARCH
SUNDAY
MONDAY
TUESDAY
WEDNESDAY
THURSDAY
FRIDAY
SATURDAY

APRIL
SUNDAY
MONDAY
TUESDAY
WEDNESDAY
THURSDAY
FRIDAY
SATURDAY

MAY
SUNDAY
MONDAY
TUESDAY
WEDNESDAY
THURSDAY
FRIDAY
SATURDAY

JUNE
SUNDAY
MONDAY
TUESDAY
WEDNESDAY
THURSDAY
FRIDAY
SATURDAY

JULY
SUNDAY
MONDAY
TUESDAY
WEDNESDAY
THURSDAY
FRIDAY
SATURDAY

August
SUNDAY
MONDAY
TUESDAY
WEDNESDAY
THURSDAY
FRIDAY
SATURDAY

SEPTEMBER
SUNDAY
MONDAY
TUESDAY
WEDNESDAY
THURSDAY
FRIDAY
SATURDAY

OCTOBER
SUNDAY
MONDAY
TUESDAY
WEDNESDAY
THURSDAY
FRIDAY
SATURDAY

NOVEMBER
SUNDAY
MONDAY
TUESDAY
WEDNESDAY
THURSDAY
FRIDAY
SATURDAY

December
SUNDAY
MONDAY
TUESDAY
WEDNESDAY
THURSDAY
FRIDAY
SATURDAY

all the
WONDERS
you seek
ARE WITHIN
YOURSELF
SIR THOMAS BROWNE

DAILY INSPIRATION

Illustrated words, quotes and poetry can provide visual bliss and insight for a meaningful life. This collection of inspirational designs illustrates a few of my favorite quotes to serve as gentle messages and reminders of life's goodness. These particular coloring pages are practical for making wall art for personal décor or gift giving. The coloring possibilities are endless, so you can make many versions of the art, and none will ever be the same.

- Use an inspirational coloring page to serve as a theme for each month in your home, workplace or classroom. With colored pencils or markers, color a full-sized inspiration page and display it where it is clearly visible such as on a mirror, bulletin board, door, etc.

- Make a mixed-media coloring piece with the inspirational art pages for gifts or encouragement. Mix up your coloring tools to add vibrant variety using colored pencils, markers, sparkly glittering gel pens, watercolors and even acrylic paints. Color the different areas of one page with the various mediums.

- Print multiple sizes of the designs and color the quote pages on heavier paper, like cardstock. Keep colored cards handy for giveaways for family, friends and co-workers.

Be the change you wish to see in the world
GANDHI

I am here
to LIVE
out LOUD
EMILE
ZOLA

Live
Each day
with
Passion
and Purpose

Be
Who
You Are

Do What You Love

just be.

your LIFE is your MESSAGE
EKNATH EASWARAN

Wherever
You Go,
go with
ALL Your
Heart
Confucius

You were Born to Shine

You're always had the Power
GLINDa the GOOD WITCH

all the
WONDERS
you seek
ARE WITHIN
YOURSELF
SIR THOMAS BROWNE

Love
your
awesome
life

MENU
Meal Planner
Breakfast
Lunch
Dinner
Sunday
Monday
Tuesday
Wednesday
Thursday
Friday
Saturday

PLANNING and JOURNALING

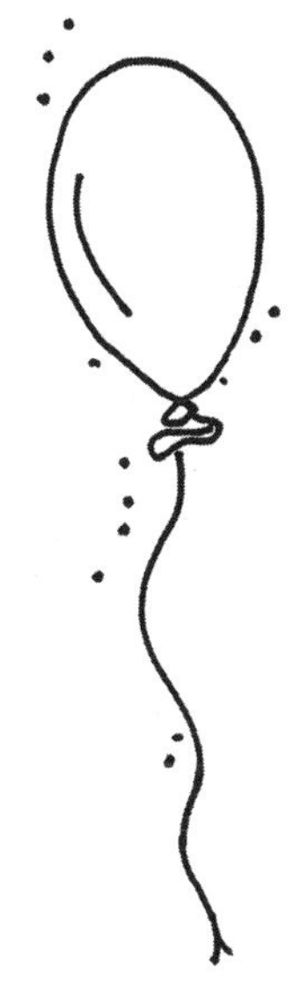

Step away from technology and handwrite the details of daily recollections and reflection. Define your life intentions. Plan special menus and celebrations on your own colorful copies of master pages ready to use repeatedly.

- Copy the master pages at full size for journaling, making a menu and listing celebrations. Have them coil-bound into a large flipbook for coloring.

- Print and color a monthly menu using four copies of the master art page. Change the look each time, coloring your planning pages with your pencils and markers using seasonal color stories and palettes.

- Make your own journals using the Sunday through Saturday art pages to document your daily life and reflect on your thoughts. Use the daily writing spaces to make volumes of gratitude journals that you can print and color over and over again.

- Have your custom journals printed and cut to any size on any type of cardstock. Have the books coil-bound and give them uncolored as gifts to teens, friends, teachers, family, etc.

- With large spaces for writing, use the weekly pages to create a daily prayer or meditation journal. Color the pages using your favorite color schemes, and use different pens for writing to add interest to the pages.

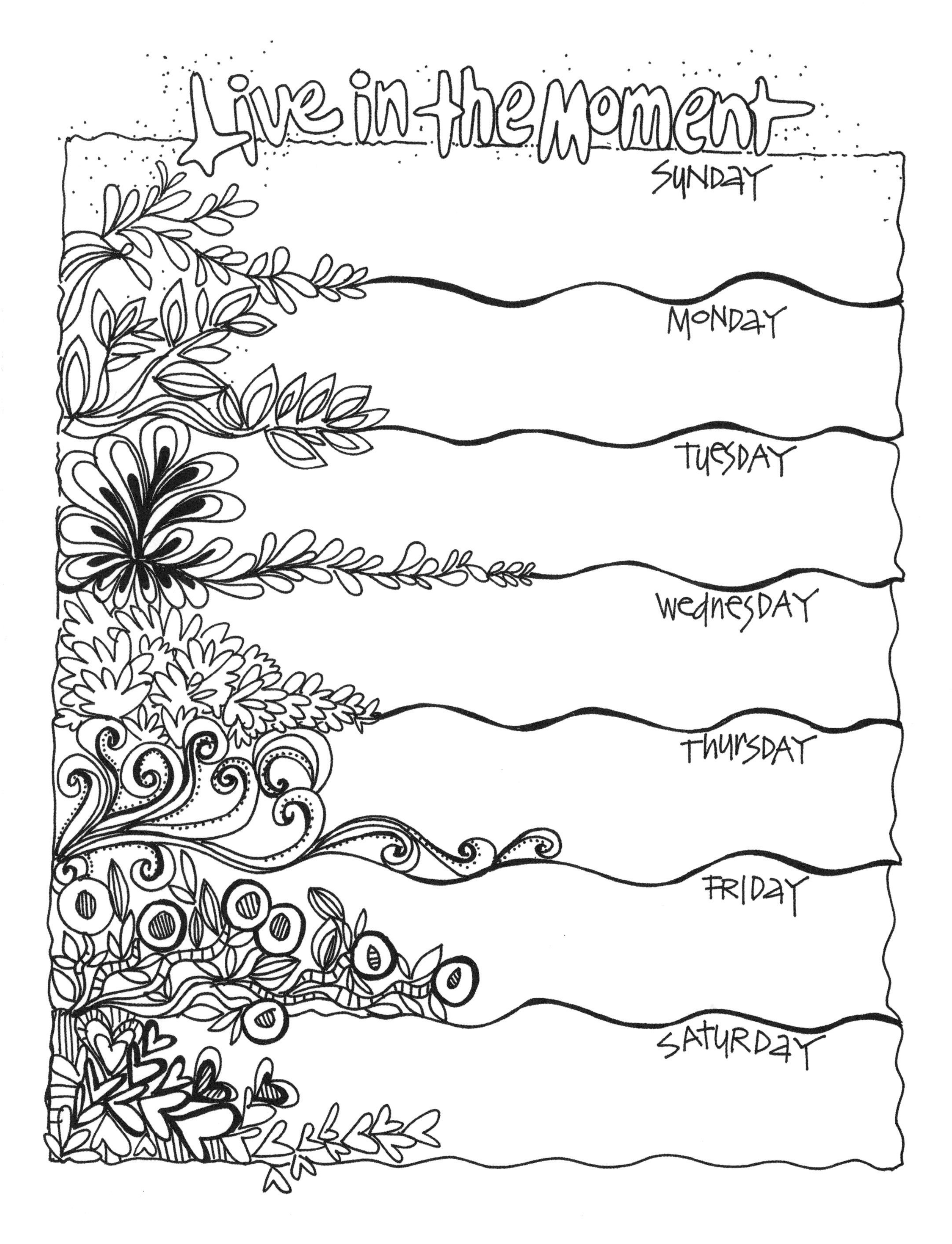

Live in the Moment
SUNDAY
MONDAY
TUESDAY
WEDNESDAY
THURSDAY
FRIDAY
SATURDAY

I love my Awesome Life
Sunday
Monday
Tuesday
Wednesday
Thursday
Friday
Saturday

TODAY'S THE DAY

SUNDAY

MONDAY

TUESDAY

WEDNESDAY

THURSDAY

FRIDAY

SATURDAY

Daily Intentions

gathering quiet thoughts....

in my heart.... my soul.... my spirit....

Celebrate!
Happy Days
January
February
March
April
May
June
July
August
September
October
November
December

MENU
MEAL PLANNER
BREAKFAST
LUNCH
DINNER
Sunday
Monday
Tuesday
Wednesday
Thursday
Friday
Saturday

DEDICATION

This book is for my colorful parents, Ronnie and Stan Zawacki. For Mom who always provided the crayons, taught me to color in the lines beautifully and aspire to perfection with pride in everything we do. For Dad, who encouraged me take those skills and live an authentic, artful life coloring outside the lines. They knew my heart, and had the perfect recipe for this daughter to live her dream as an artist.

 Published by North Light Books, an imprint of F+W Media, Inc., 10151 Carver Road, Suite 200, Blue Ash, Ohio, 45242. (800) 289-0963. First Edition.

Other fine North Light Books are available from your favorite bookstore, art supply store or online supplier. Visit our website at fwmedia.com.

20 19 18 17 16 5 4 3 2 1

Distributed in Canada by Fraser Direct
100 Armstrong Avenue
Georgetown, ON, Canada L7G 5S4
Tel: (905) 877-4411

Distributed in the U.K. and Europe
by F&W Media International LTD
Brunel House, Forde Close, Newton Abbot, TQ12 4PU, UK
Tel: (+44) 1626 323200, Fax: (+44) 1626 323319
Email: enquiries@fwmedia.com

ISBN 13: 978-1-4403-4911-9

Edited by Tonia Jenny
Interior designed by Jared Fetters
Production coordinated by Jennifer Bass
Photography by Zenna James

JOANNE SHARPE

Joanne Sharpe is an energetic, whimsical artist dedicated to empowering women to embrace their creativity through online classes and traveling workshops that explore artful sewing, journaling, hand-lettering, and a variety of mixed-media and textile art forms. She is the author of the best-selling title *The Art of Whimsical Lettering* (Interweave 2014), named an Amazon's Editor's Pick for a Best Craft Book of 2014. Joanne is proud to be a BERNINA Artisan Ambassador, sharing her love of threads and fabric with an audience eager to learn how to bring these expressive media into their own artwork. Look for her second book, *The Art of Whimsical Stitching*, a colorful handbook of ideas and techniques for playful art sewing. Joanne resides in Rochester, New York, with her very supportive husband, is the mom to a daughter, three sons and a first time grandma to a precious baby girl. Follow all Joanne's artful adventures at: joannesharpe.com